THE
PASSIONATE
LIFE

BIBLE STUDY SERIES

1 & 2 Timothy

HEAVEN'S
TRUTH AND
URGENCY

12-WEEK STUDY GUIDE

BroadStreet
PUBLISHING

BroadStreet Publishing Group, LLC
Racine, Wisconsin, USA
BroadStreetPublishing.com

The Passionate Life Bible Study Series
1 & 2 TIMOTHY: HEAVEN'S TRUTH AND URGENCY 12-WEEK STUDY GUIDE

Copyright © 2016 The Passion Translation®

Edited by Jeremy Bouma

ISBN-13: 978-1-4245-5335-8 (soft cover)
ISBN-13: 978-1-4245-5336-5 (e-book)

To purchase any of the study guides in the The Passionate Life Bible Study Series in bulk for use in groups, please send an email to orders@broadstreetpublishing.com.

Cover design by Chris Garborg at GarborgDesign.com
Typesetting by Katherine Lloyd at theDESKonline.com

Printed in the United States of America

16 17 18 19 20 5 4 3 2 1

Contents

Using The Passionate Life Bible Study

The psalmist declares, "Truth's shining light guides me in my choices and decisions; the revelation of your Word makes my pathway clear" (Psalm 119:105).

This verse forms the foundation of The Passionate Life Bible Study series. Not only do we want to kindle within you a deep, burning passion for God and his Word, but we also want to let the Word's light blaze a bright path before you to help you make truth-filled choices and decisions, while encountering the heart of God along the way.

God longs to have his Word expressed in a way that unlocks the passion of his heart for the reader. Inspired by The Passion Translation but usable with any Bible translation, this is a heart-level Bible study, from the passion of God's heart to the passion of your heart. Our goal is to trigger inside you an overwhelming response to the truth of the Bible.

DISCOVER. EXPLORE. EXPERIENCE. SHARE.

Each of the following lessons is divided into four sections: *Discover the Heart of God*; *Explore the Heart of God*; *Experience the Heart of God*; and *Share the Heart of God*. They are meant to guide your study of the truth of God's Word, while drawing you closer and deeper into his passionate heart for you and your world.

The *Discover* section is designed to help you make observations about the reading. Every lesson opens with the same three questions: What did you notice, perhaps for the first time? What questions do you have? And, what did you learn about the heart of God? There are no right answers here! They are meant to jump-start your journey into God's truth by bringing to the surface your initial impressions about the passage. The other questions help draw your attention to specific points the author wrote and discover the truths God is conveying.

Explore takes you deeper into God's Word by inviting you to think more critically and explain what the passage is saying. Often there is some extra information to highlight and clarify certain aspects of the passage, while inviting you to make connections. Don't worry if the answers aren't immediately apparent. Sometimes you may need to dig a little deeper or take a little more time to think. You'll be grateful you did, because you will have tapped into God's revelation-light in greater measure!

Experience is meant to help you do just that: experience God's heart for you personally. It will help you live out God's Word by applying it to your unique life situation. Each question in this section is designed to bring the Bible into your world in fresh, exciting, and relevant ways. At the end of this section, you will have a better idea of how to make choices and decisions that please God, while walking through life on clear paths bathed in the light of his revelation!

The final section is *Share*. God's Word isn't meant to be merely studied or memorized; it's meant to be shared with other people—both through living and telling. This section helps you understand how the reading relates to growing closer to others, to enriching your fellowship and relationship with your world. It also helps you listen to the stories of those around you, so you can bridge Jesus' story with their stories.

SUGGESTIONS FOR INDIVIDUAL STUDY

Reading and studying the Bible is an exciting journey! This study is designed to help you encounter the heart of God and let his Word to you reach deep down into your very soul—all so you can live and enjoy the life he intends for you. And like with any journey, a number of practices will help you along the way:

1. Begin your lesson time in prayer, asking God to open up his Word to you in new ways, show areas of your heart that need teaching

and healing, and correct any area in which you're living contrary to his desires for your life.

2. Read the opening section to gain an understanding of the major themes of the reading and ideas for each lesson.

3. Read through the Scripture passage once, underlining or noting in your Bible anything that stands out to you. Reread the passage again, keeping in mind these three questions: What did you notice, perhaps for the first time? What questions do you have? What did you learn about the heart of God?

4. Write your answers to the questions in this Bible study guide or a notebook. If you do get stuck, first ask God to reveal his Word to you and guide you in his truth. And then, either wait until your small group time or ask a trusted leader for help.

5. Use the end of the lesson to focus your time of prayer, thanking and praising God for the truth of his Word, for what he has revealed to you, and for how he has impacted your daily life.

SUGGESTIONS FOR SMALL GROUP STUDY

The goal of this study is to understand God's Word for you and your community in greater measure, while encountering his heart along the way. A number of practices will help your group as you journey together:

1. Group studies usually go better when everyone is prepared to participate. The best way to prepare is to come having read the lesson's Scripture reading beforehand. Following the suggestions in each individual study will enrich your time as a community as well.

2. Before you begin the study, your group should nominate a leader to guide the discussion. While this person should work through the questions beforehand, his or her main job isn't to lecture, but to

help move the conversation along by asking the lesson questions and facilitating the discussion.

3. Encourage everyone to share. Be sure to listen well, contribute where you feel led, and try not to dominate the conversation.

4. The number one rule for community interaction is: nothing is off-limits! No question is too dumb; no answer is out of bounds. While many questions in this study have "right" answers, most are designed to push you and your friends to explore the passage more deeply and understand what it means for daily living.

5. Finally, be ready for God to reveal himself through the passage being discussed and through the discussion that arises out of the group he's put together. Pray that he would reveal his heart and revelation-light to you all in deeper ways. And be open to being challenged, corrected, and changed.

Again, we pray and trust that this Bible study will kindle in you a burning, passionate desire for God and his heart, while impacting your life for years to come. May it open wide the storehouse of heaven's revelation-light. May it reveal new and greater insights into the mysteries of God and the king-dom-realm life he has for you. And may you encounter the heart of God in more fresh and relevant ways than you ever thought possible!

Introduction to 1 and 2 Timothy

The words in 1 and 2 Timothy, given from a spiritual father to his spiritual son, are powerful words for our churches today. They are letters written by Paul to help pastors and leaders bring order and appoint elders for their churches. In fact, Timothy was an apostolic apprentice to Paul, a spiritual father who poured into his life, even after being sent out to establish churches and bring them to maturity.

The clear purpose of 1 Timothy is to reveal and emphasize the glorious truths of God. False teachers had begun to infiltrate the church of Ephesus, and Timothy was given the mission of preserving the truth and cleansing the church of error.

The book of 2 Timothy could be called the last will and testament of Paul the apostle. Filled with warnings of the troubles that were ahead, this letter speaks to our generation with an unusual urgency. Paul's heart burns as he looks to the end of his journey and knows that death is near. He stirs our conscience with his emotional letter.

We've designed this study to help you explore and discover God's heart for you, the church, and the world through heaven's urgent truths. Explore them with a hungry heart, wrap them around your life, and watch God bring true growth and maturity into your spirit. May you be strengthened in grace to be faithful to run your life's race with passion and love to the very end!

The Worst of Sinners Captured by Amazing Grace

1 TIMOTHY 1:1–20

I can testify that the Word is true and deserves to
be received by all, for Jesus Christ came into the world
to bring sinners back to life—even me, the worst sinner of all!
Yet I was captured by grace. (1 Timothy 1:15–16)

The song "Amazing Grace" is probably the most famous of all Christian hymns. It also perfectly captures the essence of today's lesson and the urgent, practical revelation-truths that unfold through 1 and 2 Timothy: "Amazing grace, how sweet the sound that saved a wretch like me! I once was lost, but now am found, was blind, but now I see."[1]

This was John Newton's story. It was also the story of the apostle Paul, who was captured by God's amazing grace even though he was "the worst of sinners" (1 Timothy 1:15). Paul revealed that this grace had cascaded into his life "so that Jesus Christ could display through me the outpouring

---

1   John Newton, "Amazing Grace," 1779, public domain.

of his Spirit as a pattern to be seen for all those who would believe in him for eternal life" (1 Timothy 1:16).

What we discover in this lesson on urgent, practical Christian truth is that Jesus, the Anointed One, came into the world to bring wretches back to life. As a result of God's mercy-kiss, our lives have been flooded with such incredible grace that we overflow like a swelling river, full of faith and love!

Discover the Heart of God

- After reading 1 Timothy 1:1–20, what did you notice, perhaps for the first time? What questions do you have? What did you learn about the heart of God?

- What do deceptive doctrines and false teachings promote and breed? What power are they devoted to?

• How had some believers in Ephesus been led astray?

• Paul was commissioned by God to preach the wonderful news of Jesus. Yet he was a very different person beforehand. How did Paul describe who he was before he was "kissed" by mercy and captured by amazing grace?

• Why did Jesus come into the world? How was this purpose displayed in Paul's life?

Explore the Heart of God

- Why was it so crucial that Timothy discipled the believers in Ephesus, teaching them not to follow certain errors? How do deceptive doctrines and misleading teachings lead Christians astray, and what is the danger?

- What is "the Law," and what was its purpose? How does it identify the people in 1 Timothy 1:10? Why is the Law for them?

- Paul said, "Mercy kissed me," and he was "flooded with such incredible grace" (1 Timothy 1:13–14). Describe those events of Paul's life, as recounted in Acts 9:1–31.

• What does it say about the heart of God that Paul said, "Jesus Christ came into the world to bring sinners back to life—even me, the worst sinner of all" (1 Timothy 1:15)? What does it say about God's heart that God saved Paul to display through him "the out-pouring of his Spirit as a pattern to be seen for all those who would believe in him [Jesus Christ] for eternal life" (1 Timothy 1:16)?

• What does it mean to be "destitute of the true faith" (1 Timothy 1:19)? What does it look like to fall away in such a manner as Hymenaeus and Alexander did?

Experience the Heart of God

- Do you have a spiritual child in the faith, like Paul had with Timothy? Or are you a Timothy to a Paul? How have either of these spiritual roles deepened your experience of the heart of God?

- Paul was very concerned about the false, deceptive doctrines that were promoting and breeding controversy in the Ephesian church. What kinds of deceptive doctrines threaten your experience of the amazing-grace heart of God?

- Like Paul, all of us have a story—we were kissed by mercy and flooded with incredible grace. What is your story? What was your initial experience of the heart of God?

• What is your response to being "captured by grace" (1 Timothy 1:16)? Is it one of constant praise? Take time to let your "praises rise to the King of all the universe," using 1 Timothy 1:17 as a guide.

• How can you hold on to faith and guard against falling away as others have?

Share the Heart of God

• Whom might you disciple, as Paul did Timothy, to make them spiritual children and draw them closer to the heart of God?

- Do you know people who have been or might be "led astray by misleading teachings and speculations that emphasize nothing more than the empty words of men" (1 Timothy 1:6)? What would it look like to share the heart of God with them to keep them in the faith?

- Paul declared that Jesus came to us to bring sinners back to life. Who in your life needs to know this amazing-grace good news? How might it look to share the heart of God with them?

CONSIDER THIS

"Amazing grace, how sweet the sound that saved a wretch like me! I once was lost, but now am found, was blind, but now I see." This is our story as much as it was John Newton's and Paul's. Mercy kissed us, even though we were blasphemers and rebellious wretches. May we respond as Paul did: by letting our praises rise to the King of all the universe!

A Lesson on Prayer and Worship

1 TIMOTHY 2:1-15

Most of all, I'm writing to encourage you to pray with gratitude to God. Pray for all men with all forms of prayers and requests as you intercede with intense passion. (1 Timothy 2:1)

The books of 1 and 2 Timothy have been dubbed the pastoral epistles because they offer practical, pastoral instructions on various aspects of the Christian life. In the last lesson, we began with the bedrock teaching of God's amazing grace through Jesus. Paul continues with the first in a series of practical instructions—beginning with prayer and worship.

Paul instructs us to pray "with all forms of prayers and requests as you intercede with intense passion" (1 Timothy 2:1). But these prayers aren't limited to our friends and family; they are for *all* people—even politicians! And these prayers aren't only for safety and provision but for everything we need. Men are called to offer such prayers "with hands lifted to God in worship with clean hearts, free from frustration or strife." Women are to pray "with clean hearts, dressed appropriately and adorned modestly and sensibly" (1 Timothy 2:8-9).

One of the most important insights we discover is the revelation-truth that when we pray, we pray to Jesus, for no one else is the Mediator between God and people. So pray to Jesus on all occasions with intense passion and gratitude to God!

Discover the Heart of God

- After reading 1 Timothy 2:1–15, what did you notice, perhaps for the first time? What questions do you have? What did you learn about the heart of God?

- How does Paul say we should pray? Whom should we pray for?

- According to 1 Timothy 2:4, how many people does God want to embrace his saving life?

• How does Paul say men and women should and shouldn't act, especially when it comes to prayer and worship? In particular, how should women act who are new to the faith?

Explore the Heart of God

• Paul said one of the main reasons he wrote 1 Timothy was to encourage believers to "pray for all men with all forms of prayers and requests as you intercede with intense passion" (1 Timothy 2:1). How do you suppose that looks practically? Why is it pleasing to Christ when we pray for people—especially leaders?

• What does it mean and why is it significant that "there is one Mediator between God and the sons of men—the true man, Jesus, the Anointed One" (1 Timothy 2:5)?

- What does Paul mean when he says that Jesus "gave himself as ransom-payment for everyone" (1 Timothy 2:6)? What was this act, and what did it do for us?

- Read 1 Timothy 2:8–15 again. Paul instructing women to "learn in quietness" means he wanted them to take the respectful posture of a disciple in this new way of worshiping the true God. When Paul urged them not to be teachers, he was referring to their old religious system, where women were the temple leaders and teachers of the goddess religion in Ephesus. How should this teaching inform and shape how men and women act in the church today, particularly when it comes to prayer and worship?

Experience the Heart of God

- Consider your prayer life. Does it reflect how Paul says we should pray in 1 Timothy 2:1–4? What about 1 Timothy 2:8–14?

- What does it mean to you that Jesus, the Son of God, died by giving himself as a ransom-payment for you (1 Timothy 2:6)? How should this realization impact your experience of the heart of God?

- Paul's instructions in 1 Timothy 2:8–14 have been a hotly discussed passage relating to men and women. How do you think it would impact your experience of the heart of God when it comes to prayer and worship to take these teachings seriously?

Share the Heart of God

- Paul instructed us to pray with gratitude and to pray for all people with all kinds of prayers (1 Timothy 1:1). This is one way you can share the heart of God with people in your life. So do that now. Spend time lifting up those you know before the throne of God.

- How often do you pray for your political leaders and representatives? Paul said, "It is pleasing to our Savior God to pray for them" (1 Timothy 2:3). Spend some time right now praying for those who lead your country and city.

- Paul declared that there is "one Mediator between God and the sons of men" (1 Timothy 2:5) and that God desires all to experience his heart of saving lives. How should this affect your sharing of God's heart with those you know?

CONSIDER THIS

Paul invites us to offer up all kinds of prayers and petitions before the throne of God with reverence and modesty. Here is a prayer you can pray, the prayer of our Lord Jesus:

Our Father, dwelling in the heavenly realms,
may the glory of your name
be the center on which our lives turn.
Manifest your kingdom realm,
and cause your every purpose to be fulfilled on earth,
just as it is fulfilled in heaven.
Give us today the bread of tomorrow.
Forgive us the wrongs we have done as we ourselves
release forgiveness to those who have wronged us.
Rescue us every time we face tribulation
and set us free from evil.
For you are the King who rules
with power and glory forever. Amen. (Matthew 6:9–13)

Lesson 3

———

Qualifications for Those Who Serve the Church

1 TIMOTHY 3:1–16

If any of you aspires to be an overseer in the church, you have set your heart toward a noble ambition, for the Word is true! Yet an elder needs to meet certain qualifications. (1 Timothy 3:1–2)

The last lesson contained practical insights on Christian prayer and worship. Today's offers practical instructions on Christian leadership. Paul was concerned about "the affairs of the church of the Living God" (1 Timothy 3:15). So he laid out a number of qualifications for the two main positions of local church leadership: overseers and deacons.

Also called "elders" or "bishops," overseers *oversee* the teaching ministry of the church, functioning as pastors. Paul calls this leadership role "a noble ambition" (1 Timothy 3:1) and insists that anyone who aspires to it must be self-controlled, the spouse of one person, respectable, hospitable, a capable teacher, gentle, a peacemaker, and not a lover of worldly possessions.

Deacons function as servants to the people and to the organizational aspects of a local church. A deacon must be worthy of respect, not indulgent in the things of the world, truthful, a guardian of the faith, a spouse to one partner, a faithful manager of his household, and he must serve the church well.

Have you set your heart on the "noble ambition" of leading God's people, either as an overseer or deacon? Discover what God desires from his leaders and consider how you might help conduct the affairs of the church, the very household of God.

Discover the Heart of God

- After reading 1 Timothy 3:1–16, what did you notice, perhaps for the first time? What questions do you have? What did you learn about the heart of God?

- There are a number of terms that are synonymous for *elder*, such as *pastor, shepherd, presbyter, bishop, overseer,* or *guardian.* Paul set out a number of qualifications for those who aspire to be such a leader. List them here.

- Paul also listed a number of requirements for deacons. What are they?

- The word used in 1 Timothy 1:11 for "women" may refer to female deacons. Phoebe is called a deacon in Romans 16:1. What are the requirements of women leaders in the church?

- How did Paul describe the church in today's lesson?

- What or who is the "mystery of righteousness" (1 Timothy 3:16)? How did Paul describe this "mystery"?

Explore the Heart of God

- What are the roles of an overseer or elder in the church? How about a deacon?

- Why do you think each of the requirements for church leaders you listed in questions 2 and 3 of the previous section are so important? What does it tell you about the heart of God for his church and his people that he has such strict requirements for leaders?

- Why do you suppose Paul had special instructions for women in 1 Timothy 3:11? Why are each of the qualifications important?

- In what way is the church of the Lord God "his very household, the supporting pillar and firm foundation of the truth" (1 Timothy 3:15)?

- First Timothy 3:16 describes the son of God, Jesus Christ. In what way was he a "mystery"?

Experience the Heart of God

- Who among the church leaders you know best exemplifies the qualifications Paul outlined in 1 Timothy 3:1–13? How have they furthered your experience of the heart of God?

- If you aspire to church leadership, how do the qualifications outlined in 1 Timothy 3:1–13 shape your understanding of leading God's people? Of the qualifications for church leadership, which speak to you the most? Are there any you lack? Explain.

- Have you ever known or heard stories of church leaders who were given a position of authority and didn't meet the qualifications in this lesson? What was the result, and how did they impact your experience of the heart of God?

Share the Heart of God

- Consider again Paul's qualifications for church leaders. How do they enable such leaders to help people experience the heart of God?

- If you are a church leader, God has called you to a high standard of living for the sake of his love-mission in the world. How can you better serve those around you in order to share the heart of God?

- What does it mean for sharing the heart of God with the world that the church is the living God's "very household, the supporting pillar and firm foundation of the truth" (1 Timothy 3:15)?

CONSIDER THIS

Perhaps you've never given much thought to the structure and leadership of your church, but Paul says it's vital, a worthy and noble ambition. Why? Because every local church is the very household of the living God, "the supporting pillar and firm foundation of the truth" of God (1 Timothy 3:15). How might God want to use you to care for his people and support his truth?

Lesson 4

———

Train in a Way That Brings Lasting Benefit

1 TIMOTHY 4:1–16

Be engaged in the training of truth that brings righteousness.
For athletic training only benefits you for a short season,
but righteousness brings lasting benefit in everything.
(1 Timothy 4:7–8)

Paul opens our lesson with a shot across the bow that hits painfully close to home: "At the end of this age, many will depart from the true faith one after another, devoting themselves to spirits of deception and following demon-inspired revelations and theories" (1 Timothy 4:1).

From "gospels" that promise financial blessing to teachings that reimagine sexuality and hell, it seems as though the fundamental teachings about the one true faith are fraying at the edges. Which is why we need this lesson on a third practical Christian truth: discipleship.

Discipleship carries with it the idea of training in a way that brings lasting benefit in believing and living. Perhaps that's why Paul used the metaphor of athletic training to encourage us to "be engaged in the training of truth that brings righteousness." But, as in every kind of training, we're encouraged to "be quick to abstain," in this case "from senseless traditions and legends" (1 Timothy 4:7).

Paul urges us today to give as much attention to the way we live, how we believe, and what we teach as we do to train for a marathon. So consider how you are training in the truth that brings righteousness!

Discover the Heart of God

- After reading 1 Timothy 4:1–16, what did you notice, perhaps for the first time? What questions do you have? What did you learn about the heart of God?

- What has the Holy Spirit explicitly revealed about the end of the age? List all that he reveals in this passage.

- What kind of reputation did Paul promise that Christian leaders would have if they teach what the Holy Spirit reveals? In what ways should Christian leaders nurture other believers?

- From what should Christians be quick to abstain? With what should they have nothing to do? What should they engage in and do instead?

- To what did Paul urge Timothy and other Christians to give careful attention? What would be the result of such attention?

Explore the Heart of God

- Why do you think it's important for Christians to teach what the Holy Spirit revealed in 1 Timothy 4:1–5? Why will a teacher "be known as a faithful and good minister" for teaching them?

- Paul spoke of abstaining "from senseless traditions and legends" (1 Timothy 4:7). What was he speaking about here? Why is "truth that brings righteousness" an antidote to such teachings?

- Paul said athletic training has short-term benefits, but righteousness has long-term benefits. What does Paul mean by that? What are these benefits?

- Why should Christian leaders, especially young ones, not be intimidated by older believers? Why should their focus instead be on the example Paul outlined in 1 Timothy 4:12?

- How does it look practically to do what Paul instructed in our reading (to be diligent in devouring the Word of God, to be faithful in prayer and teaching believers, to attend to our spiritual life, and to live what we preach)?

Experience the Heart of God

- The Holy Spirit through Paul revealed several characteristics of the end of the age, the time before Christ's return. How have these revelations already come to pass in our age?

- What "senseless traditions and legends" do Christians need to abstain from today?

- Paul spoke of training in righteousness and godliness having more benefit than physical training. Do you train in godliness the same way you train physically? How might doing so impact your experience of the heart of God?

- How would it look in your life to "be diligent in devouring the Word of God, be faithful in prayer, and in teaching the believers" (1 Timothy 4:13)? How would it look to "give careful attention to your spiritual life and every cherished truth you teach" (1 Timothy 4:16)? How would this practice deepen your experience of the heart of God?

Share the Heart of God

- The Holy Spirit has revealed in our reading that at the end of the age, many Christians will depart from the true faith. How can you share the heart of God with those you know to nurture and help preserve their faith?

- Paul urged us to engage in "the training of truth that brings righteousness" (1 Timothy 4:7). Part of training is coaching others to do the same. Who can you help train?

- How might it look to toil tirelessly for someone in your life in the same way Paul toiled because of his "hope in the Living God" (1 Timothy 4:10)? How can you be diligent in teaching other believers the way of righteousness?

- Paul said that one way we share the heart of God is by giving careful attention to how we live—spiritually and in the world. How do you need to pay attention to your spiritual life and way of living in order to "release even more abundant life inside you and to all those who listen to you" (1 Timothy 4:16)?

CONSIDER THIS

While our physical bodies need strict training to build muscle and endurance, our spiritual "bodies" need as much training to build spiritual muscle (truth) and spiritual endurance (righteousness). So form a training plan for yourself and consider training others in the truths of the faith. After all, the righteousness that results from such training "contains the promises of life, for time and eternity" (1 Timothy 4:8)!

Lesson 5

Proper Treatment of Fellow Believers

1 TIMOTHY 5:1–6:2

The church needs to honor and support the widows,
especially those who are in dire need. . . . The pastors who lead
the church well should be paid well. (1 Timothy 5:3, 17)

Paul continues his series of practical revelation-truths for Christian living by turning our attention to the topic of honor and support of fellow believers in the household of God. Four separate groups are at the center of Paul's instructions: age groups, widows, church leaders, and employers.

First, Paul says that we are to honor both older people and younger people by treating them with encouragement and purity. From there he launches a lengthy exhortation on properly honoring and supporting widows. In Paul's day, women obtained their status and social identity from men, so a woman who lost her husband would be left without any support. That's where the church family came in. Paul lays out specific instructions for how the church should care for widows—even insisting that believers who don't take care of their own are compromising their faith! He ends with a lesson on properly treating two other groups: church leaders and employers.

In the end, honoring and supporting these beloved members of God's family is a way in which we faithfully honor our sacred obligation to God himself!

Discover the Heart of God

- After reading 1 Timothy 5:1–6:2, what did you notice, perhaps for the first time? What questions do you have? What did you learn about the heart of God?

- How did Paul urge Timothy to treat older men and women? How about younger ones?

- How should the church treat widows? How should Christians determine such treatment?

- How should pastors and other church ministry leaders be treated? Why did Paul say churches should take care with ordaining such leaders?

- What instructions did Paul have for employees—both of believers and unbelievers?

Explore the Heart of God

- Why do you think Paul spent so much time instructing Christians to honor and support widows? What does this tell us about the heart of God?

- Why is it so important that believers support their own needy family members? How is such support and provision linked to their faith?

- Paul seemed to offer pastors and other ministry leaders much support in 1 Timothy 5:17–20. Why do you suppose such support is vital for the church?

- What does Paul say about the truth of good and bad works? What does he mean, and how does it relate to both this reading and the letter as a whole?

- Why is it so important for Christian employees to honor their employers, especially believers? What impact does that have?

Experience the Heart of God

- Consider your treatment of older and younger men and women. How might it look in your life to reflect the heart of God found in 1 Timothy 5:1–2?

- Who in your family is struggling and in need of provision? How could you provide for their needs in order to experience the fullness of the heart of God?

- Paul said the truth of our ways—whether good or bad—will eventually get out. How would your ways be "recognized and acknowledged" (1 Timothy 5:25)?

Share the Heart of God

- It is clear from 1 Timothy 5:3–16 that God cares deeply for widows. Do you know any? How can you partner with God's own love-mission to share his heart with them?

- Paul has a clear love for pastors and other ministry leaders and calls us to share God's heart with them in practical and personal ways. How can you ensure that your pastors are provided for and trusted in your church?

• Our attitude as employees gives our employers "a clear testimony of God's truth and renown" (1 Timothy 6:1). How are you respecting and honoring your employer? How can you work for your supervisors in a way that shares the heart of God with them?

CONSIDER THIS

Paul reminds us that the yardstick of our faith is our honor and support for believers, especially those in need—whether widows, family members, or pastors. The apostle James echoes these urgent revelation-truths: "True spirituality that is pure in the eyes of our Father-God is to make a difference in the lives of the homeless, orphans, and widows in their troubles" (James 1:27).

Lesson 6

Persevere in the True Faith, Spiritual Fruit, and Trust

1 TIMOTHY 6:3–21

I instruct you before the God of Resurrection Life...
that you follow this commission faithfully with a clear conscience
and without blemish until the appearing of our Lord Jesus,
the Messiah. (1 Timothy 6:13)

What comes to mind when you hear the word *perseverance*? "Dogged determinism" is one definition. A practical example is a woman who finished a marathon after she sprained her ankle halfway through. That's what Paul urges us to do at the close of his first letter to Timothy, in three practical areas of our Christian life.

First, we are called to persevere in the true faith. Paul warns that people who teach what is contrary to the truth prove they know nothing at all. This is why he advises, "Distance yourself from them and their teachings" (1 Timothy 6:5). Then he calls for perseverance in spiritual fruit. He instructs Timothy to "chase after true holiness, justice, faithfulness, love, hope, and tender humility" (1 Timothy 6:11), the true produce of our Spirit-life. Finally, we are called to persevere in trusting "the one who has lavished upon us all good things, fulfilling our every need" (1 Timothy 6:17), rather than trusting in the riches of this world.

Discover from these revelation-truths the strength you need to faithfully finish your life's race with perseverance and passion, and to "fight with faith for the winner's prize" (1 Timothy 6:12).

Discover the Heart of God

- After reading 1 Timothy 6:3–21, what did you notice, perhaps for the first time? What questions do you have? What did you learn about the heart of God?

- How did Paul describe people who teach contrary truths and doctrines? How do they affect others? How did Paul say believers should respond to those who teach such contrary truths?

- What happens to people who crave the wealth of this world? According to Paul, how does money affect people and their faith?

- Instead of running toward the spiritual error that comes from false teachings and money, toward what are we called to run with perseverance? What are we to chase after?

- In what did Paul instruct Timothy "before the God of Resurrection Life" (1 Timothy 6:13) before Paul closed his letter? About what did Paul want Timothy to remind and command certain people in the world?

Explore the Heart of God

- Paul had strong words for those who teach "other doctrines that are contrary to the truth" (1 Timothy 6:3). Why do you suppose that was? Why is such teaching so harmful to people's experience of the heart of God?

- Why do false teachings and doctrines "add misery to many lives by corrupting their minds and cheating them of the truth" (1 Timothy 6:5)? Why is it so important to distance ourselves from false teachings and doctrines and instead to persevere in the truth of our faith?

- Why do people who crave wealth "slip into spiritual snares" (1 Timothy 6:9)? Why is the love of money the root of all kinds of evil and "the first step toward all kinds of trouble" (1 Timothy 6:10)?

- Why should believers run from the two big troubles Paul warned against: false teachings and the love of money?

- How does it look to "fight with faith for the winner's prize" (1 Timothy 6:12)? How does it look to follow Christ's commission regarding our lives "with a clear conscience and without blemish until the appearing of our Lord Jesus, the Messiah" (1 Timothy 6:14)?

Experience the Heart of God

- What "doctrines that are contrary to the truth" (1 Timothy 6:3) are being taught today? How should you respond so that you fully experience the heart of God?

- How have you witnessed the love of money and the craving of wealth lead people to all kinds of evil? How did these things impact their experience of the heart of God?

- Do you crave or love money and wealth? How can you guard against both to safeguard your experience of the heart of God?

- How do you think it looks in your life to "fight with faith for the winner's prize" and "lay your hands upon eternal life" (1 Timothy 6:12)?

- What can you do to not "forget all that has been deposited within you" (1 Timothy 6:20)?

Share the Heart of God

- Do you know people who are following after doctrines contrary to the truth of Christianity? How can you share the heart of God by helping them leave those doctrines behind and persevere in the truth?

- Do you know people who crave wealth and are in love with money? How might it look to share the heart of God by sharing with them "the meaning of true life" (1 Timothy 6:19)?

- What can you do to help Christians in your life remember all of the revelation-truths of the faith that have been deposited within them?

CONSIDER THIS

Paul ends the first handful of practical insights into Christian living by urging us to never "forget all that has been deposited within you" (1 Timothy 6:20). Though others who have claimed to possess revelation-knowledge have wandered from the true faith, in both beliefs and practices, may you persevere in your calling, eventually laying your hands on the prize: eternal life!

Lesson 7

Rekindle the Fire of Your Spiritual Gift

2 TIMOTHY 1:1–18

*I'm writing to encourage you to fan into a flame and rekindle
the fire of the spiritual gift God imparted to you when
I laid my hands upon you.* (2 Timothy 1:6)

This lesson opens the second letter Paul wrote to his protégé Timothy, imparting words of counsel and warning. You could call it the apostle's last will and testament, because it is filled to the brim with important revelation-truth, insights that speak to our generation with an unusual urgency. As he looks to the end of his journey, Paul knows that death is near. His heart burns for Christ and for his disciples, and he stirs our conscience with his emotional letter. It begins with a charge to guard the good deposit of our faith that has been entrusted to us.

Sometimes we need that encouragement, don't we? Between carting the kids around to school and practice, working our nine-to-five jobs, and mowing the lawn and raking leaves, it can be difficult to keep the fire of our faith burning bright and strong. Yet Paul invites us to rekindle the fire of the spiritual gift imparted to us.

When we do, not only will our faith and love for the Anointed One grow even stronger, but we'll also be convinced "that he is more than able to keep all that I've placed in his hands safe and secure until the fullness of his appearing" (2 Timothy 1:12).

Discover the Heart of God

- After reading 2 Timothy 1:1–18, what did you notice, perhaps for the first time? What questions do you have? What did you learn about the heart of God?

- How did Timothy's faith begin? How did it progress?

- Why did Paul write Timothy this second letter? What was he encouraging him to do and to guard?

• Paul said we've been given the Holy Spirit. Rather than being a "spirit of cowardly fear" (2 Timothy 1:7), what does the Holy Spirit do for us?

• What truth about Jesus and our life in him "is now being unveiled" (2 Timothy 1:10)? What has our Life-Giver done for and given to us?

Explore the Heart of God

• What is "the wonderful promise of life found in Jesus, the anointed Messiah" Paul mentioned at the beginning of 2 Timothy 1:1?

• Why did Timothy need to "fan into a flame" (2 Timothy 1:6) the spiritual gift God gave him? What does it look like to rekindle our faith?

- Why do you think Paul gave Timothy the reminder in 2 Timothy 1:7? What is "the spirit of cowardly fear"? How does it contrast to the Holy Spirit?

- Paul spoke of grace having been given to us before time began. How is this the case? What is this grace, and why isn't it something we get by any good works?

- Why is it that Paul was able "to overcome every difficulty without shame" (2 Timothy 1:12)? What was it about Paul's faith that convinced him that God was "more than able to keep all that I've placed in his hands safe and secure until the fullness of his appearing" (2 Timothy 1:12)?

• What is the treasure we and Timothy are called to guard well? How does the Holy Spirit help us?

Experience the Heart of God

• Paul spoke of Timothy's faith being passed along to him through two people: his grandmother and his mother. Who passed along your faith to you? Who has been instrumental in your experience of the heart of God?

• Paul urged Timothy to fan into flame his spiritual gift. Do you need the same "fanning" and "rekindling"? If so, how? Why?

- Do you struggle with fear? How can 2 Timothy 1:7 encourage you and your experience with the heart of God?

- What do you need to do in order to "guard well this incomparable treasure by the Spirit of Holiness living within you" (2 Timothy 1:14)? Make a list of two or three practical things, commit to doing them, then ask the Holy Spirit to empower you.

- Have you ever been "ashamed of the testimony of our Lord" (2 Timothy 1:8)? What was that experience like? How can 2 Timothy 1:8-10 encourage your experience of the heart of God?

Share the Heart of God

- Paul said he was appointed by God "to announce the wonderful promise of life found in Jesus, the anointed Messiah" (2 Timothy 1:1). How would it look in your life to take Paul's mission as your own? To carry out God's plan of salvation laid out in the Bible by sharing the heart of God with those around you?

- Paul spoke of others passing along to Timothy a "strong faith" (2 Timothy 1:5). How would it look in your life—as a parent or grandparent, a relative or friend—to share the heart of God with others by following the example of Lois and Eunice?

- *Fear* is such a small word for such a big emotion. Whom do you know who needs the encouragement of 2 Timothy 1:7? Make an effort this week to show and share the mighty power, love, deliverance, protection, and security of the heart of God.

- Instead of shame over the testimony of our Lord, we're called to show and share him. With confidence in your calling, how might it look in your life to unveil the revelation of your Life-Giver to those you know?

CONSIDER THIS

Our times are urgent times, as they were for Timothy in Ephesus. Paul recognized this, which is why he wrote this urgent letter, encouraging his faith and infusing his ministry with revelation-truth. As Paul realized, our own urgent times mean we dare not let the fire of our faith dwindle and flicker out! What steps can you take to rekindle your faith's fire?

Lesson 8

Endure and Overcome for the Sake of Christ

2 TIMOTHY 2:1–15

*Carefully consider all that I've taught you, and may
our Lord inspire you with wisdom and revelation in everything
you say and do. But make Jesus, the Anointed One,
your focus in life and ministry. (2 Timothy 2:7–8)*

How does it look to endure the Christian life? To overcome the struggles of living the lives we've been called to live in Christ? Endurance and overcoming is the theme of today's lesson. Using a cast of characters, Paul teaches us what it means to endure as a Christian and overcome every form of evil.

First, Paul exhorts us to "overcome every form of evil as a victorious soldier of Jesus the Anointed One" (2 Timothy 2:3). He compares our Christian life to a soldier who's been called to active duty. A soldier leaves behind civilian affairs in order to please his commanding officer; we're called to do the same. Then there's the athlete. If he doesn't play by the rules, he will never receive the trophy; neither will we. Finally, there's the hardworking farmer, "who labors to produce a crop [and] should be the first one to be fed from its harvest" (2 Timothy 2:6).

Do you see the correlations? Life as a Christian takes sacrificial denial, self-discipline, and hard work—all for the sake of Christ. And when we do endure and overcome, Paul promises we will reign triumphantly!

Discover the Heart of God

- After reading 2 Timothy 2:1–15, what did you notice, perhaps for the first time? What questions do you have? What did you learn about the heart of God?

- How did Paul call on Timothy to live his life? How did Paul call on Timothy to overcome evil and suffer hardships as a Christian?

- What three metaphors did Paul use to illustrate the Christian life?

- What is the reason Paul was "persecuted and imprisoned by evildo-ers" (2 Timothy 2:9)? Why did he endure such hardship?

- What words could Timothy trust about Jesus's death and life, his suffering and triumph?

Explore the Heart of God

- How is it that we live our Christian life "empowered by God's free-flowing grace" (2 Timothy 2:1)?

- Paul told Timothy to pass along "all that you've learned from me" (2 Timothy 2:2). What was it he had learned? What was he to pass along?

• Paul used the metaphors of a victorious soldier, an athlete, and a farmer to talk about the Christian life. Explain how these metaphors relate to overcoming evil and joining Paul in suffering for Christ.

• What did Paul mean by these trustworthy words: "If we were joined with him in his death, then we are joined with him in his life" (2 Timothy 2:11)?

• How is it that even though we are faithless, Jesus is still faithful? What does this tell us about the heart of God?

Experience the Heart of God

- What practical steps can you take right now to "live your life empowered by God's free-flowing grace" (2 Timothy 2:1) in order to experience the heart of God in greater measure?

- Paul likened the Christian life to a soldier who "must divorce himself from the distractions of this world," athletes who play by the rules, and a farmer "who labors to produce a crop" (2 Timothy 2:4, 6). How would it look in your life to endure and overcome like them so you can experience the heart of God?

- Consider 2 Timothy 2:8 again. Do you remember Jesus by keeping him the focus of your life and calling? If so, how can you maintain that focus? If not, what is your focus? And what can you do to remember him and keep him as your life's focus?

- Consider Paul's encouragement and warning in 2 Timothy 2:11–13 again. Have you ever been unfaithful to Jesus? What was that experience like? Recommit anew to never disregard him, delighting in the reality that Jesus "never wavers in his faithfulness to us" (2 Timothy 2:13).

Share the Heart of God

- What practical steps can you take in your life right now to pass on all that you've learned, in order to share the heart of God with those you know?

- It is clear from 2 Timothy and the entire New Testament that Paul suffered for the sake of Christ and others. How might it look to join Paul in enduring hardship so that those in your life might "discover the overcoming life that is in Jesus Christ, and experience a glory that lasts forever" (2 Timothy 2:10)?

- Read 2 Timothy 2:11–13 again. How might these words be life-giving, hopeful messages for those you know? Who can you share them with this week so that they can experience the heart of God?

CONSIDER THIS

Enduring suffering and overcoming evil might seem like an exhausting, impossible demand. Never fear, because Paul promises us something remarkable: even if we are faithless, Jesus will never waver in his faithfulness to us! So, then, "live your life empowered by God's free-flowing grace, which is your true strength, found in the anointing of Jesus and your union with him" (2 Timothy 2:1).

Lesson 9

God Knows His Own, His Own Forsake Wickedness

2 TIMOTHY 2:14–26

*But the firm foundation of God has written upon it these
two inscriptions: "The Lord God recognizes those who are
truly his!" and, "Everyone who worships the name of the
Lord Jesus must forsake wickedness!" (2 Timothy 2:19)*

Today's lesson revolves around two inscriptions written upon God's
firm foundation: "The Lord God recognizes those who are truly his" and
"Everyone who worships the name of the Lord Jesus must forsake wickedness" (2 Timothy 2:19). In other words, God knows his own, and his own
must forsake wickedness.

These inscriptions are an urgent clarion call for believers because, as we
will learn in this lesson, they speak about the need to confirm our election in
Christ as God's children. To explain, Paul uses the illustration of a palace with
containers and utensils of gold and silver, wood and clay. As Paul explains in
our reading, we must transform from being everyday vessels of wood and clay
into being containers of gold and silver that are "dedicated to the honorable

purposes of your Master" (2 Timothy 2:21). How do we prepare ourselves in this way? Here's a sample: avoid meaningless arguments and worthless words, and run from the evil desires of youth to pursue righteous ones.

Those who are God's very own worship only him, and his heart beats for them in recognition. Discover and explore in this lesson how to be only his and truly his!

Discover the Heart of God

- After reading 2 Timothy 2:14–26, what did you notice, perhaps for the first time? What questions do you have? What did you learn about the heart of God?

- What did Paul want Timothy to commit himself to reminding and warning God's people about? What did Paul want him to do his best to eagerly pursue? How about avoid?

- How did Paul describe the words of Hymenaeus and Philetus? Why were they guilty?

- What does the firm foundation of God have written upon it?

- From what did Paul instruct Timothy to flee and stay away? What did he want him to chase and be instead?

Explore the Heart of God

- What did Paul mean by "empty chatter and worthless words" (2 Timothy 2:16)? How are those words like gangrene or spreading poison?

- How can the kind of chatter and words Paul spoke about in 2 Timothy 2:16–18 be subversive to believers' faith? Can you name any modern examples?

- What is the firm foundation Paul referenced in 2 Timothy 2:19? Why are the two inscriptions so significant to that foundation and our faith?

- Paul used a metaphor of a palace with containers and tableware. Explain what he meant. How did it relate to the Christian life and faith?

- What are the "ambitions and lusts of youth" (2 Timothy 2:22)? What is the pure thing Paul wanted Timothy to pursue instead?

- Why did Paul want Timothy to stay away from "foolish arguments" (2 Timothy 2:23)? Can you think of any examples? How do such arguments impact people's experience of the heart of God? How does what Paul wanted Timothy to pursue affect it?

Experience the Heart of God

- What are the meaningless arguments and quarrels that rage throughout the church nowadays? How can you guard against being drawn into them?

- Have you witnessed the effects of poisonous, godless, empty chatter, especially when it comes to erroneous teaching? How might it look to avoid such chatter?

- Consider Paul's analogy in 2 Timothy 2:20–21. Which of the two articles and utensils—those used for honorable purposes or disgraceful ones—does your life reflect? How can you keep the containers of your life "prepared for every good work that [your Master] gives you to do" (2 Timothy 2:21)?

- Consider what you are pursuing: "the ambitions and lusts of youth" or "all that is pure" (2 Timothy 2:22)? How would it look to make your holy pursuit "whatever builds up your faith and deepens your love" (2 Timothy 2:22)?

Share the Heart of God

- Have you ever witnessed or participated in someone being torn down by useless words that harm? What was that like? How can you be a person who shares the heart of God instead?

- Paul was very concerned with those who spread poisonous truths and subvert people's faith. How might you work toward the opposite, teaching the firm foundation of the heart of God to those you know?

- Paul gives an important reason for us to avoid foolish arguments and immature disputes: so that we'll "be able to carefully enlighten those who argue with you so they can see God's gracious gift of repentance and be brought to the truth" (2 Timothy 2:25). How might it look in your life to, with gentleness and meekness, help others see the truth?

CONSIDER THIS

The inscription engraved on God's foundation is clear: he knows his own and his own forsake wickedness. Are you known by God as his son or daughter? Do you confess the name of the Lord? Then turn away from wickedness and worship only him. Live as a valuable vessel prepared and eager to do your Master's special work!

Lesson 10

A Warning about the Final Days

2 TIMOTHY 3:1–9

But you need to be aware that in the final days the culture of society will sink so low into degradation that it will be extremely difficult for the people of God. (2 Timothy 3:1)

It has always been challenging for the people of God to live in the world. Consider the Roman world of Paul and Timothy: babies were left for dead in a practice called exposure, sexual immorality was rampant and public, government corruption was woven into the fabric of society, and Christians were threatened for standing for truth. Sounds familiar, doesn't it?

The similarity between Paul's time and ours makes sense, because as Paul warns in today's lesson, "be aware that in the final days the culture of society will sink so low into degradation that it will be extremely difficult for the people of God" (2 Timothy 3:1). Look at how he described such days: people will love themselves with a self-centered lust, obsess about money, mock what is right, become addicted to slander, hate what is good and right, act with brutality, and delight in the world's pleasures rather than God's love.

It's no wonder Paul gave those of us who are living in the last days the same warning he gave Timothy: stay away from such people! Take heed and consider how your culture opposes and threatens the truth of God.

Discover the Heart of God

- After reading 2 Timothy 3:1–9, what did you notice, perhaps for the first time? What questions do you have? What did you learn about the heart of God?

- What will happen with the culture of society in the final days? What will people be like in the final days? List all the ways Paul describes such people.

- What will people find their pleasure in? Where will they find it?

- How will people in the final days treat God? How did Paul say Timothy and believers should treat such people? Why?

- Who are the historical examples Paul listed of the people who reject and stand against the truth of God?

Explore the Heart of God

- What did Paul mean by "the final days" (2 Timothy 3:1)? What (or when) is this?

- Why are the final days marked by such degradation?

- Have we always been in the final days? Or is 2 Timothy 3:1–4 a description of a future (or present) time?

- How might 2 Timothy 3:5 be a summary of 3:1–4? Why should we heed Paul's instruction and have nothing to do with the people he mentioned?

• 2 Timothy 3:8 is a fascinating verse, for Jannes and Jambres are never mentioned by name in Exodus. The Old Testament simply mentions the sorcerers who wanted to compete with Moses and his authority. What is Paul telling us by referring to Jannes and Jambres? How are they examples of what Paul has been saying?

Experience the Heart of God

• Do you think we are in the final days? How does our time mirror what Paul warned about in 2 Timothy 3:1–4?

• Paul said that in the finals days it will become "extremely difficult for the people of God" (2 Timothy 3:1). How does that make you feel? How might you prepare for such an experience?

- Why is Paul's advice in 2 Timothy 3:5 so important to our experience of the heart of God?

- How can we ensure that we don't become corrupt and hard-hearted in these final days, like Jannes and Jambres did?

Share the Heart of God

- Paul said that in the final days, our culture will degrade and people will have no respect for God and his ways. How might it look to be a force of salt and light during such a time?

- If you are a leader in your church, how might you help protect your people from those who worm their way into other's hearts?

CONSIDER THIS

Not only does our culture arrogantly oppose God, so do false teachers, as Paul reveals in our lesson. While our culture threatens us on the outside, false teachers threaten us on the inside. We must be vigilant in these last days to have nothing to do with such people. Thankfully, we are promised that they will not advance against the cause and kingdom of God!

———

Continue in What You Have Learned

2 TIMOTHY 3:10–17

You must continue to advance in strength with the truth wrapped around your heart, being assured by God that he's the One who has truly taught you all these things. (2 Timothy 3:14)

Who has been instrumental in teaching you and shaping your life? Who has shown you Christ's love and Christian endurance? Who has displayed remarkable faith in the face of great suffering and difficulties? Who has modeled patience with others? Who has taught you the fundamentals of the Christian faith, perhaps from childhood?

In one of his final charges to his protégé, Paul offers Timothy something most of us can relate to: an example of a sure and steady way of life. Paul was Timothy's example; he learned from Paul how to live the kind of life God calls us to live and also learned from him the content of his faith. But Paul didn't stop there. He pointed Timothy to one more sure and steady foundation for learning: the Holy Scriptures. Because, unlike Paul's own example, this one is breathed by God himself!

Today's lesson is about the sure and steady foundations for learning Christian truth and living the Christian life and then continuing in them. God uses both the example of others and his Holy Word to teach us all things!

Discover the Heart of God

- After reading 2 Timothy 3:10–17, what did you notice, perhaps for the first time? What questions do you have? What did you learn about the heart of God?

- What example of living did Paul say Timothy should closely follow? Explain.

- Whom did Paul say would experience persecution?

- Paul warned Timothy against "evil men" and "deceivers" (2 Timothy 3:13). What was his warning? What did Timothy need to do instead? What did Paul want Timothy to remember?

- When Paul wrote 2 Timothy 3:16, he was referring to the Torah and all the Old Testament writings. Today, "every Scripture" would include the New Testament as well. How did Paul describe Scripture? What is it and what does it do?

Explore the Heart of God

- Read 2 Timothy 3:10–12 again. How do you think it looked in Timothy's life to reflect and live what Paul was commending?

- Why do you think what Paul revealed in 2 Timothy 3:12 is true (that those who live for and faithfully follow after Jesus will be persecuted)?

- Explain the contrast Paul presented in 2 Timothy 3:13–14. What was Paul encouraging and warning against?

- Paul urged Timothy to "remember what you were taught from your childhood from the Holy Scrolls" (2 Timothy 3:15). What would Timothy have been taught from childhood?

- What did Paul mean that "every Scripture has been written by the Holy Spirit, the breath of God" (2 Timothy 3:16)? Why is this an important, foundational belief to our faith? And why is it crucial to what Paul said in the rest of the verse and in 2 Timothy 4:17?

Experience the Heart of God

- Is there anyone you know whose experience of Christian love, endurance, patience, and perseverance you can follow and mirror—just as Timothy did with Paul? If so, who? Explain.

- What do you think about the idea that "all who choose to live passionately and faithfully as worshipers of Jesus, the Anointed One, will also experience persecution" (2 Timothy 3:12)? How might such living and persecution impact your experience of the heart of God?

- While Paul warned against evil men and deceivers leading people from truth, he also encouraged advancement in strength and truth. How would it look in your life to "continue to advance in strength with the truth wrapped around your heart" (2 Timothy 3:14)?

- All Scripture is God-breathed, which means that the Bible is God's book—one that should shape every ounce of our life. How do you need to continue letting the Bible instruct, correct, rebuke, and train you in order to experience the heart of God in increasing measure?

Share the Heart of God

- How might it look to be a Pauline example for a Timothy in your life? To love and endure by not giving up? To express faith and hunger for the things of God? To have patience with others and endure persecution as a model for someone you know?

- Consider again Paul's warning against evildoers and imposters of Christianity who lead people from the faith. How can you do the opposite: stand on the truth of Scripture and lead people toward the faith and heart of God?

- It's clear there were people in Timothy's life from a very early age who poured themselves into his life and faith. How might it look for you to impart the wisdom of the faith to the young people you know and share the heart of God with them?

CONSIDER THIS

The Christian life can be an exhausting and confusing one, which is why we need both the examples of saints and the Word of God. What have you learned from the people in your life who have modeled the way of Christ? What have you learned from the breath of God, who has equipped you for every good work? Now continue in both until the day of Christ!

Lesson 12

———

Fight the Excellent Fight

2 TIMOTHY 4:1–22

I have fought an excellent fight. I have finished my full course and
I've kept my heart full of faith. There's a crown of righteousness
waiting in heaven for me, and I know that my Lord will reward me
on his day of righteous judgment. (2 Timothy 4:7–8)

As you end this study, picture Paul sitting in a prison cell. He misses his wonderful disciple Timothy. Their love is deep, their commitment to the gospel is powerful, their desire to see the world reached with the love of Christ is real, and time is running out. But Paul had one final word for Timothy that's sure to challenge your faith and deepen your experience of the heart of God.

The essence of this final word is the center of this letter: the Word of God. Paul urges us to preach it in the full expression of the Holy Spirit, whether convenient or not; to stand on it, no matter what; and to teach it with patient endurance. He warns us that people won't care what teachers say about the Word unless it tickles their ears and lines up with their desires. Like Timothy, we're called to fight the most excellent fight by being alert to these trends, overcoming them, and carrying in our hearts the passion of our gospel-calling.

Even though Paul was abandoned by others, he fought the good fight. Yet he wasn't alone. And we aren't either, for the Lord stands with us, empowering us to complete our calling in him.

Discover the Heart of God

- After reading 2 Timothy 4:1–22, what did you notice, perhaps for the first time? What questions do you have? What did you learn about the heart of God?

- What were Paul's final instructions to Timothy?

- Paul spoke of a coming time when a number of things would become a reality in people, especially in regards to truth. What did Paul warn against?

- Paul also spoke of a coming end to his life that was "fast approaching" (2 Timothy 4:6). What did he say about his life?

- As an itinerate preacher carrying the Word of God, Paul was dependent upon others. He was also abandoned and betrayed by people—some of the very people he was dependent on. Whom did he describe to Timothy, and what did they do? Despite the fact that other people "ran off and abandoned" (2 Timothy 4:16) Paul, who stood with him? What did he do for Paul?

Explore the Heart of God

- As some final instructions, Paul urged Timothy to proclaim the Word, stand upon it, preach when it was and was not convenient, and do it all in the full expression of the Holy Spirit. How do you suppose it looked for Timothy to follow this instruction?

- Read 2 Timothy 4:3–5 again. What kind of situation did Paul describe? Why do you think such a situation would arise in the world?

- What did Paul mean that "the time is fast approaching for my release from this life and I am ready to be offered as a sacrifice" (2 Timothy 4:6)? Why could he have said what he did in 2 Timothy 4:7–8? What does the end of verse 8 tell us about the heart of God?

- What do Paul's words about those he mentioned in 2 Timothy 4:9–15 teach us about people and support—especially when it comes to ministry and truth?

- Paul contrasted those who abandoned him with the Lord, who stood with him. Explain what had happened. How do you suppose Paul felt? What does it reveal about the heart of God that the Lord stood with Paul?

Experience the Heart of God

- Paul urged Timothy not only to boldly preach God's Word but also to "stand upon it no matter what" (2 Timothy 4:2). Describe how that might look in your life, and explain how it would deepen your experience of the heart of God.

- Paul spoke of a time when people would no longer listen to truth—they would deny it and selfishly confirm their own truths and ways of living. How can you "be alert to all these things and overcome every form of evil" (2 Timothy 4:4) so you can guard your experience of the heart of God?

- Paul made an interesting claim about his life as he looked toward the end of it: "I have fought an excellent fight. I have finished my full course and I've kept my heart full of faith" (2 Timothy 4:7). Can you say the same about your life? Explain. Why might Paul's description be such a good goal and benchmark for your own experience of the heart of God?

- Have people ever abandoned you as they did Paul? Can you empathize with his experience? Explain. How should 2 Timothy 4:17–18 inform and deepen your experience of the heart of God?

Share the Heart of God

- In 2 Timothy 4:1–2, Paul spoke of sharing the heart of God with boldness, courage, and perseverance. How might it look in your life to follow what he instructed here? Why are "wisdom and patience" (2 Timothy 4:2) so crucial to instructing and teaching people and sharing the heart of God?

- Read 2 Timothy 4:3–5 again. Do you think Paul's description fits our own time? If so, how might this create barriers as well as opportunities to sharing the heart of God?

- In 2 Timothy 4:9–16, Paul spoke of being abandoned by others in his ministry. Consider those who serve your church or the ministries you're involved with. How might it look to reflect the steadfast, supportive heart of God in 4:17–18 instead?

CONSIDER THIS

Reading this chapter, you can't help but sense an urgency to Paul's final instructions for his partner in ministry. The same urgency about the Word and the world is true for us as well. May your heart burn with the Holy Spirit's fire of urgency, and may you be strengthened in grace to faithfully finish your life's race with passion and love.

Encounter the Heart of God

The Passion Translation Bible is a new, heart-level translation that expresses God's fiery heart of love to this generation, using Hebrew, Greek, and Aramaic manuscripts and merging the emotion and life-changing truth of God's Word. If you are hungry for God and want to know him on a deeper level, The Passion Translation will help you encounter God's heart and discover what he has for your life.

The Passion Translation box set includes the following eight books:

Psalms: Poetry on Fire

Proverbs: Wisdom from Above

Song of Songs: Divine Romance

Matthew: Our Loving King

John: Eternal Love

Luke and Acts: To the Lovers of God

Hebrews and James: Faith Works

Letters from Heaven: From the Apostle Paul (Galatians, Ephesians, Philippians, Colossians, I & II Timothy)

Additional titles available include:

Mark: Miracles and Mercy
Romans: Grace and Glory
1 & 2 Corinthians: Love and Truth
Letters of Love: From Peter, John, and Jude (1, 2 Peter; 1, 2, 3 John; Jude)

thePassionTranslation.com